INTO YOU

Books by Andrew Greig

POETRY

White Boats (Garret Arts, 1972)

Men On Ice (Canongate, 1977)

Surviving Passages (Canongate, 1982)

A Flame in Your Heart, with Kathleen Jamie
    (Bloodaxe Books, 1986)

The Order of the Day (Bloodaxe Books, 1990)

Western Swing (Bloodaxe Books, 1994)

MOUNTAINEERING

Summit Fever (Century Hutchinson, 1985)

Kingdoms of Experience (Century Hutchinson, 1986)

FICTION

Electric Brae (Canongate, 1992)

The Return of John MacNab (Headline Publishing, 1996)

When They Lay Bare (Faber, 1999)

That Summer (Faber, 2000)

Andrew Greig

◊

INTO YOU

BLOODAXE BOOKS

Copyright © Andrew Greig 2001

ISBN: 1 85224 555 7

First published 2001 by
Bloodaxe Books Ltd,
Highgreen,
Tarset,
Northumberland NE48 1RP.

www.bloodaxebooks.com
For further information about Bloodaxe titles
please visit our website or write to
the above address for a catalogue.

Bloodaxe Books Ltd acknowledges
the financial assistance of Northern Arts.

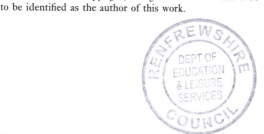

Cover printing by J. Thomson Colour Printers Ltd, Glasgow.

Printed in Great Britain by
Cromwell Press Ltd, Trowbridge, Wiltshire.

To the beloved ELN

Hallelujah to the ghosties
and all the scary monsters beneath the boiling seas

VIC CHESNUTT

Acknowledgements

Some of these poems have appeared in *The Honest Ulsterman*, *Pocketbooks*, *Poetry Scotland*, *The Scotsman*, *Shore Poets Anthology*, *The Times Literary Supplement*, and a couple of places I forgot to record.

I thank the Scottish Arts Council for the fact that for once after many years of support I have no need to thank them.

Contents

INTO YOU

Vow

Leave before dawn
with two embraces:
one that slays,
one that resurrects.

Go home now
while it's still there,
your man and your children still sleeping.

In your shaky hand
the flame that burns no fuel,
the bowl that's always brimming.

Bear it carefully through this world.
Let nothing spill.
Let there be no tears, not a drop.

Resonator

I think I like the unplucked string best
– so taut a thought between us
sets it humming.

Some days you waken to a life
as though a phone was always ringing.
How do you take that call?
(It's no surprise that phone wire
binds our hands so well.)

From time to time I hear my name
resonate though no one's spoken

one might suppose the soul
a wind–chime

shaken by a stray vibration.

A Shuttered Lantern

And when she goes she takes with her
a shuttered lantern.

Wherever you think of her inhabiting –
work, her children, bars
and friends – stays dark.
The light falls only on her face
as you last saw it.

And when she writes she must learn
to make love to him with more attention,
do more than follow the motion of his kiss,
you blink at the first glimpse
of a light that will blind you
when she raises the lamp's sides
and vanishes.

Freefall

She would say to discover
the true depth of a well –
drop a stone,
          start counting.

She means, I think, best not discuss it.

Lovers rise past my eyes in the dark.
Since she dropped me there's been
much heavy breathing in the kitchen,
delicate understandings in the hall,
kisses like promises of light
on the way down to the basement.

She hugs me kindly at the party,
I hear you've been having
quite the time.
I grin and don't know where to put my hands
for I am falling, and it's been years,
and I've heard nothing yet.

She Could Say No
(but she don't really want to)

Desire isn't wrong, only painful,
she says. (It's that torn
but centred woman once again.)
Is a chrysalis warm-blooded,
do you think it is appropriate
to kiss me now?
Beneath her shoulders
heather creaks like a pepper-grinder.

We are not helpless, only habitual
as something like a butterfly is born
improbably high on the slopes of Ben Wyvis.

Lucky
(for Lesley)

Certainly I've been lucky. Always a lover
since I left home, stayed night or weekend
but never the week. This chanced
so often it must have been willed.
That one who spoke and meant it
of intimacy so tight her ribs would fit
inside mine – little wonder she was eloquent
sensing the cage I breathed within!

I don't know how it happened
but now the factor knows my name
I have the run of man's estate.
Though the river is not what it was,
the brown and silver fish still flicker,
the hills still make me rise and sweat.
In the orchard now at summer's end
sweet and bitter fruit fall alike to earth.

Lie in bed, eyes open to the dark
while her breathing shifts the sheet
back and forward tinily across my chest.
Feel them fall, the fruit of thirty years
of love and loss, truths and delusions;
feel them come home and lie
on the thick, soft ground of my life
with only the slightest of bruising.

Tales of the Flood

A Small Emergency

You look great like that, leaving.
And you know it – face averted,
hair flopping down just so.

It brings the best of you out
like an indolent lifeguard
now sprinting across the beach...

Secretly we love it,
how loss, that undertow, drags out to sea
all sweetness, froth and scum.

Late

But it is too late: she weeps,
he weeps, in different lands.
Now another dips her head and licks
the wet back of his hand.

I'm late, she said. *Ten days now.*
Spring snow lay deep on the hill,
melt ran over their feet
where they stood, water filling their shoes.

I've never been this late.
He took her hand, they walked on
looking at the end of winter.
Their feet fell exactly where they fell

and for an hour in this life
they saw everything, perfectly well.

After the Flood

My heart's high-water mark.

When the flood recedes:
mopping, debris and stink.

No need for plaques.

Improbably high,
here comes the stain.

A Little Flood

It rains a great deal, the fields
widen and shine. It helps to remember
times when banks gave the river
momentum, when life was shaped
by a lover's walk.

She holds me lightly as we talk:
You're dearer to me than my hands,
as all my friends are dear.
I smile past her shoulder and agree
these days friends are our family.

Rain stotts off the pavement,
spraying up towards our eyes.
Somewhere the life we never led
walks through fields, holding a child
that can never grow up or die.

Down by the Riverside

Standing under trees in light
rain, end of winter, more than
half way through my life.

Thought, movement,
the pauses in between...

The swollen river lips
the bank, the branches bead
and something stops.
It comes clear: time
doesn't flow, it drips.

And here's eternities between the drops.

Citizen

I am not a citizen but a subject
and Scotland is British
like hashish is illegal and
we've both been married.

These are facts
but mean nothing
in this yellow room
as you, my English lover,
remind me of my rights (none)
then stub out the roach.

We move closer and resume
across the disputed border of this bed,
eyes shining like discarded
armour in the sun.

D., Swimming

She jumped from bed and ran
(we'd been arguing too long)
along the jetty, dived.
Silence rippled out and swam.

She came back shivering,
weed in her hair,
mud between the toes I dried.
Her mouth opened, nothing came.

Wet wool sweater thrown to the floor,
skin cold as bark, that hipless girl
rubbed with me until
our bodies shook like leaves.

Perhaps I think too much of sex,
that garment we're left holding
while pale and furious love
dives away from us in the dark.

Puritans

She's quit smoking, but still keeps
ash-tray, lighter, full pack
by her bed. A shrine to desire.
Weird shit or what.

'I can imagine everything with you
and that's enough. To know
we could love and like and grow,
talk, be silent, some evenings

watch an easy video
or have the most astounding sex.
But I'm Puritan as hedonist:
to yearn forever, that's the best.'

I light up on the stair down.
Sometimes the stuff we stuff back
in an overnight bag
is all that's needed for a life.

Combine

A man driving to his father's bedside
gets stuck behind a combine.
The harvester is red and obviously
at the end of summer
it's only natural.
He knows if his father wasn't dying
the combine would still be in the road.

The woman stands in a grocer's
by the fruit in a polka dot dress,
testing a mango and thinking
of leaving her husband.
It occurs to her the price of exotic fruit
won't be affected either way.

They have not met yet.
He fidgets at the wheel,
she squeezes the mango.

*

He drives his father's car
to their new home, down open roads.
She is coming from the shops
with a brisk sea wind
pressing polka dots to her legs.

On the whole they are glad.
He sees the fields are bare again,
she tastes fruitiness in her breath.
They know about the red combine,
they understand the cost of sweetness.

They are cradled in the pans
of an invisible balance
at the time the fat sun sets

to let a half moon rise.

Ripe

(for Eddie & Shirley)

For one, realisation came with a pebble
clicking on a bamboo fence.

With another, a fish ate shadows
when birds passed overhead.

For him perhaps a backfire
before the car key turns.

For her it comes as she sits
clicking red nails by the pink guitar.

*

In the middle of the night
I grow heavy and ache –

I could be among
a summer orchard

ripening at the tip
of a branch of your love.

A Night Rose

There's an old balance in the conservatory of the soul...
ERZEBET SZANTO

When her moment came
she cried out and handed it to me:
a Night Rose.

Black and radiant as the centre of an eye.

It rests now on
an unreachable shelf.
I think we put it there.

From time to time she writes
she's felt another petal fall.
She would not have me say where.

Petal for petal, magic and loss:
let them for once
weigh the same with us.

A Woman in Fife

Weave of her sweater tickling my cheek,
my breath in her throat's hollow.
We are holding up and letting go each other.

Light drains to slits above the rigg,
moon's up, the stars will follow.
Wings of geese beat out *So what so what?*

and the tracks of our ending are furrows
cut across winter fields
where power lines fizz into dusk.

Her Heart

(in memory of Alex Watson)

Not that loyal pump
but a cobble street
leading through mist
to a canted Council lamp,
a half-forgotten square –

hazed and empty at this hour
but still a public space
in earshot of the sea
where her ancestors gather
to greet and circulate;

their slate-grey faces
shine in the salty rains
and though they never
speak of it they bear
love deeper than her pain.

Into You

Eager, wary, hopeful, suspicious, ready to engage, she came in
leaning forward slightly
    as though pushing into a current only she sensed. When she
    glanced – one brief stare then away – her blue iris was hazed
like a windscreen when a stone hits and the driver struggles not to
panic and to hold her line. As we talked her face looked too young
for her children
    but I saw the skin on the back of her hands had taken a
beating.
    When her fingers came together to make her point, I felt them
steeple in my chest.

The first time she unbuttoned her shirt, straightened her
shoulders, looked at me
    in a spirit of free enquiry reminiscent of the early scientists
once they'd cut free of theology and the Greek philosophers and
looked upon Nature as it really was – I felt that I
was looking not so much at her small hopeful breasts
    (though they were fine, being two, being hers)
as on Nature as it really was, unspeakably on my side, and when
she smiled
    then bent, my heart was truly in her mouth.

There are days now I feel myself a field spread open to the
wind. Where she grazes all is renewed and joy is valid on the earth
we will return to, here in the body's each trembling blade.

ORRA POEMS (I)

orra: n, Scots: abnormal, peculiar, vagrant, casual
orra-man: n, odd-job man, esp. rural

In the Frozen Nursery

In the frozen nursery there is a pain
that never ceases, never hurts, a fine
facsimile of pain – useful, transparent,
to real pain as rice-paper is to parchment.
The books which line the nursery
are dummies mostly, whose bindings front
some piddling secret – a bottle, letters,
a work of amateur pornography.

Outside the window, the fields of your birth
are white with snow, featureless
as the woman leaning on the hours
you cannot concentrate. She proffers
life in miniature: a toy piano,
a tiny bed, a blonde & minute doll –

a happiness no bigger than your thumb.

       *

In the frozen nursery an imaginary child,
delighted, earnest, with tremendous care
is stalking an imagined mouse
along the patterned carpet border
between sleep and wide-awake.
Somewhere in the haunted house
a piano repeats an unresolvable tune...
A whiff of Brylcreem, urine, trouser-stain,
I have him now. It is the orphan boy
who came one Christmas,
to whom we must be kind, and weren't,
who for days at the piano chased
the one tune till he lost it in tantrums, tears...

Boy, I've played that tune for thirty years.

       *

The nursery is thawing, it must be spring.
Now whatever books remain are hung
upon the greening trees outside; their secrets rise
in streams of smoke from chimneys.
Snow creaks on the roof, the snowman
slumps. Out in the garden
a full-sized woman turns and waves,
the mouse squeals to be released –

I slide the window up and leap,
one falling shriek

                 into the world.

A Pre-Breakfast Rant

Dull, dull, hungry cloth-head dullard! Each day
I'm dull, even this ache is dull (though fatal). Each night
I climb on my lover and we ride
nowhere we haven't been before.
Dull the knife, dull the mirror,
dull each pane of glass around us.
Nothing here is sharp, clear or dangerous,
and even you, my blood's sugar, have plummeted.
Let me stand at the window once more and stare
till the world's no longer *out there*.

True world, where are you hiding? Whose crime
makes you hide so? Is it the light yet murderous
force of habit, settling like dust on the mirror,
that makes you slip away?
The world is hid behind itself, smirking slightly,
as though we're in a murder mystery
where the killer and the clue are right in this room
and we're looking (for God's sake, they can be nowhere else!)
the way I looked at you last night on the floor
and could not see what I saw before...

Open up, true world! I'm banging on
your pane that you might open
or shower down daggers and cut me to ribbons.
I can bear anything but this dull that I am.
This cloth I've somehow spread over the world,
when I open my eyes
may it be whipped away. Reveal again
the morning laid like a shining breakfast table
with as many places as there are appetites
for this day to – truly – begin.

(Aside)

Oh but it is no longer possible
to start or end with exclamation!
You add it is in poor taste to write
as though language were not the only possible subject of language
as it bows over itself, spilling its seed.

And these poems are but memorials to moments
like when we sat in the scullery, talking in low voices,
and sunlight through dirty side windows
inched up pale hairs on your arm, drowning each
in honey till I bent to suck such transcience!

But when our palms turn upwards and flop
on the sheets, and spectral figures move
caught in an urgency we do not feel,
and we become untethered –
what else will have weight with us

but these moments in sun or in rain,
happy or unhappy, with a face turning our way,
and what else but these will we emit at the end
like dry ice rising about the heart, the head,
to mask our exit, even from ourselves?

That Summer
(when modernist met theory queen)

The flesh she sat in, like a glowing robe
worn casually to go about the world in,
required no ornament, had none.
No bangles, paints, rings, or unguents.

So she thought and rocked that summer,
naked as virtue in the hammock
beneath the vines in broken light.
The mesh raised faint welts on her skin
as she improvised on discourse, the Other,
the text redoubled, slidey signifiers,
all that French Quarter jazz – to me,
deaf to anything but her!

    'I love cats, causes and analysis.
    This other love you urge is suspect,
    founded on the bourgeois construct
    of the self, who as we know
    is not Mrs, Miss or Ms – but myth.
    How can you possibly say you love me?'

Ah, the way she turned
sentences and her head alike
with an upward questioning turn!
She came in from the garden,
her arms full of veg
and her head full of critical theory,
quoting Lacan, Benjamin, Foucault,
while I chopped onions and logic.
Sometimes those mealtimes brought
a little water to the eyes.

    'But desire obscures its object
    like a fist raised to the sun.
    How can you know me that way?
    This is not the way to know me.'

And, whispered in the night,

> 'I say *Je t'aime* – the foreign language
> because this feeling's strange to me.'

One scared to feel, the other
loath to reconsider –
through prickly days and sticky nights
we ran our summer seminar
on difference of thought and gender...

Ach well. Without her I never would have gained
my Doctorate in Higher Objectivity.
I concede feeling's no excuse, and 'love'
the slipperiest of all discourses.
Yet now, when all our words
are dust along the whispering gallery,
I do not give a monkey's for those thinkers.

Memory has its tides, and now the waters
tilt back to thoughtless parting lips,
her serene and gracious nod that summer
as she, the theory queen, at last inclined
and head met body in the shower.

TA-TA

A Small White Dog

And when we die, they say,
a small white dog
trots into the big dark wood,
to do his business.

Or a woman steps from her dress,
walks along the broken jetty
to the end then dives
through light to liquid light.

I'm waiting on the bank
to see where she will reappear,
listening to a muffled bark
from the heart of the wood.

Their Last Bow

Though it might be asking for it
and it's not very Scottish
let's admit we're happy now.

They can take it away from us
and from time to time we will
take it away from each other

but for this matinee we hang
suspended from our disbelief,
acting lovers' flight to the hilt.

We cannot love too much
you say in a stage whisper
before we uncouple from that clutch

where we become one on the floor
and hold it as though that,
not death, was the final act.

Beloved let us hold hands as we rise
to face the world in its blaze of lights.
I hear bells no one has shaken, and sense

the white noise of Being applauding itself
for merely turning up on the night.
How can we know till it falls

how much the show's shaped by its final curtain
or whether we'll step back through it
once, twice, hands clasped high

as we take our last bow
before we disappear
with an exhausted, radiant salute?

Stair

Only one life and it's now,
she decided as she crossed the yard,
thumped her shoulder to the outer door.
One leg in sunlight, one in shade,
she carried something in her arms
– split logs, books, a lazy pup –
whatever the moment had delivered.

She got the news
as she passed through
the scullery. No one moved
when she pushed past brother, father,
the silent doctor on the stair
cupping a cigarette on his way down,
along the landing to the final room.

Surely she entered, looked, and saw,
but someone with something in her arms
keeps climbing stairs that rise
past endless corridors of light.
I am lost, she thinks, *unchained.*
It's time to be very afraid.
She climbs dry-eyed, her shoulders braced.

What we carry at such times
defines who we are now,
she claims. At the wake she seemed
to have winged heels – at least,
while she danced, her mother's bracelet
glittered blue and gold
around her ankle, just above the bone.

A Royal Visit

Preparing for Death or Life –
same procedure
whether it's the King or Queen
comes calling.

Keep your doorstep clean,
the interior uncluttered,
kettle on the boil, a simple spread
of goodies close at hand,
something savoury, something sweet.
A clean towel for the occasion,
some light reading in the loo.

A quick call-by is all they demand.
Leave your door open
so they won't break it down.
Now, make like you're not waiting.

An Investigation

What has passed here
to freeze the cursor,
wipe so clean the answering tape?
This chair aligned precisely to its desk,
the gaping microwave, a well-stocked fridge,
the pack of condoms by the bed...

Lower your eyes, those slooshing cans.
You are standing in the epicentre
of a non-event so absolute
there's no one left to question:
no victim, witness, not even a child
hiding in a room upstairs.

Perhaps that is the crime,
for something in the unscribbled walls
and the underlying order, as it were, implies
though women have passed through
(photos of holidays, weddings, friends' babies)
there never have been children here.

Peaceful, certainly. It could be
the life of a gay man, but it's not.
Take a seat, make coffee, eat the last
slightly stale rock bun
as you check your notes and reach
the only possible conclusion.

Now pour the petrol of this yearning,
throw down your burning cigarette and go.

Swarm

(for Marjory)

When her husband stopped breathing
she unfolded her hands,
noted the time like a good doctor
then rose to kiss his eyes –

she saw fuzzy lines of specks
(something between a hexagram
and a highly organised swarm)
rise past the yellow radiator,

move through the glass,
expand then vanish in the sky.

*

These days she cries
her short fierce greit
only on anniversaries.
I hold her till it's done.

The hour on his certificate
is wrong, she says – I took
some secret time before I left
and that I share with no one.

She smiles, sits up in bed:
It's a beautiful day, I fancy
croissants and café au lait.

But what about that swarm?
Don't think about it, she replies,
it doesn't matter. Yet.

*

We breakfast on the terrace
at the end of summer:
the coffee bites, the knife
spreads light like honey.

Here's such a thing
as love that endures
even its own helplessness.
She looks up, laughs

into a speckless sky.

Norman's Goodnight

One drops
in a bunker.
Another on his doorstep,
Christmas morning, shovelling snow.

When I go
may it be like that,
a short fall down and out
while busy in open air

like a pigeon
winging it across clear sky
curves then plummets,
brought down by stray buckshot.

And may there be time
to murmur as I fold
some brief word of thanks
and letting go –

like the last time I saw MacCaig
standing at his door;
as I turned the stair
his hand came up, waved:

Ta-ta. Ta-ta.
Masterly concision –
thank you and
goodnight in one.

I hope to be
even briefer as I fall:

        Ta –

ORRA POEMS (II)

Glider

Surely the river runs more clearly here today
when I write with absolute calm
of river gnats clinging to the underside of leaves –

Happiness! I mind it fine
that spring I built and launched my glider
watched it rise against the sun,
and saw right through that dream
to its perfect skeleton

as it soared, circled, descended, stuck
high in the beech above the river.
I threw sticks to bring it down
and carried it home smashed on a morning
much like this, still and insect-ridden.

Today I'm sitting by that water
working on something where
everything is as I say it is

and the problem's how to make that stick
when that tree blew down years back
and was cut into rounds
one of which lies yet in my lover's back garden
while through the hole in its core

yellow-orange nasturtiums pour wild and free.

Watch The

Saw bird on top branch
round sunset. It chirruped
not to me, not to itself,
it just sang lots:
time for sleep, or soft fuck off.

Ten years back, wrote about
such bird as sang like that.
I'd been cut open for a spell,
sad case haemophiliac
couldn't stop bleeding
till I stopped   right there:
felt the moment clot.

This sings like linty. Wrong
again. It doesn't sing
like anything. Beak snapped open,
black bird gives free-form aria
to deepening shades et cetera...

It sings, I stand, it hangs
branch against sky – a steep
moment in February.
Momentum stops, bird is
as it is, and I am,
whatever these may be.

In Borderlands

With tiny adjustments of its wings
the buzzard holds steady in the gale:
if you could live well,
it would be like that.

Over the Border
yellow lights snap on.
Draw curtains, re-tune the radio.
These constant voices...

Perhaps you are too much alone
and wonder why.

*

Take the clasp out of your hair
and try not to be fated.

Listen till you go
behind the wind.
There is nothing there
but an amazing pressure gradient.

The kettle steams, for a moment you ride
high in the gale of *I am*.
You say a name and it goes out
on wavelengths Marconi never dreamed of.

Angels

Bred by Wenders out of Rilke
they turn up everywhere
impassive or smirking slightly
invariably handsome

soaring above the marketplace
hanging round your bedroom

You might shut your door against them
yet they schmooze through walls and ceilings
like metaphysical dry rot

*

Sometimes you need to step outside
what does exist
into what does not

look back and see it whole

Yet you keep the stopper in
the perfume bottle
with good reason

Before something precious evaporates
let's bottle up for ten years
angels and other heavenly bodies

till they re-acquire shock value
and the merest whiff
puts our hearts in a spin

– like the one who leaving said
We are entering a time
of great spiritual need

And I agreed
though she had the modesty to go
on foot not on the wing

The back door blew open
now all through the house
white curtains

mime

great wings beating

Scotland

On the dreich and unfashionable
   side of the street
      at the northern edge of town

we've hunched shivering,
   blue and belly-aching
      like a hungover mendicant

by MacDiarmid out of Picasso,
   parading ribbons of our old campaigns
      that is to say, defeats –

for a few hundred years.
   And telling with a certain
      ressentiment

a pitiful tale
   though true
      if not always to the point

how we were once independent
   upright and proud
      that is, quarrelsome and prone

to beating up folk,
   often our own,
      but have since fallen on hard times.

Aye, we been robbed,
   crippled and colonised,
      blinded and generally shafted

and if we have a wee drink problem,
   who could possibly dream
      of addressing a thistle

unless he were thoroughly guttered?

Oh blethering seannachie
   skiving on the machair
      clutching mongrel polyglottal

tatters of languages
   which we once wore
      in eloquent style n'est-ce pas

and that staff we grip –
   when no one's looking
      we beat ourselves with it.

Isn't it time
   we rose now
      with our hand off our crutch –

with a new century across the way
   isn't it time
      we got up and

wobbly
   a bit light in the head
      kind of feart actually

walked clear-headed
   open-hearted
      unaided

to greet it?

HIGHLANDS & ISLANDS

Stromness Evening

(for George Mackay Brown)

Sun's sloped off across slack water,
haar wreathes the Sound of Hoy.
We could call each day a wager
but the books are closing now.

My neighbour's in his doorway
playing blues harmonica –
not that he's unhappy,
it's just what he does well;

you can tell by the manner
the notes stretch and prowl
like stray dogs long after
he's stopped – the way

a man's still thought on
as Calum knocks out his harp
and we glance, silent a moment,
at a certain dark window on our way to the pub.

Above North Ronaldsay

Down there a tractor stutters, stops;
a dog's bark is carried out to sea and lost.

A metal thermos glitters. Along the shore
the air shakes midgies where a cigarette unwinds.

A blue fleece jacket blinks
like an eye as she strips down...

The plane banks, or memory does.
Entering the clouds at summer's end,

you shift in your seat as complimentary drinks come by,
feeling the itch yet from that unlocatable sand.

Slip Knot

We're letting something pull through our hands,
almost enjoying the burn of the rope
so thick and coarse your little fist
can scarcely close round it.

Last summer, how we looped it
with one quick flick around the stanchion
as though a simple knot were a way of declaring
the sea's the same in all directions.

The clouds that slide down the Flow
on the grease of their own shadows
won't find us tied up as before
canoodling and fishing under the pier.

What were we thinking of, to let it slip?
The rope is coarse, the current strong,
we can hold on no more.
As the happy shore grows small

admit the heart beats a little faster.
In your eyes' gleam I see
the water rising under the straik.
How small this boat's become.

Last Walk in Tayinloan, Kintyre

Your last hour won't be remembered. That's
the only difference between it and any other hour.
As though you walk down to the sea

past the old blue tractor, the rusty bailer,
the collie tied with twine by the silage pit –
and simply don't come back again.

When the sky drips blue
though the wind is fresh, and yellow
runs from the sun's mouth,

the world comes breaking at your heart.
It will flow in so strongly
it displaces you

like an air bubble from a bottle.
This is the pure experience you always said you wanted.
Slump down by the path. A sweetie paper

snagged in grass is the last thing that you'll see.
You are lying on your side on the machair,
wind in your face, and believe me

regret and fear are just gulls at the far end of the bay.
The world's so full. It swells, rushes in,
rolls over you. A small pop! and you're gone...

The day is full to the brim without you
whose life was a wander no one, least of all you, can retrace.
The sun's still hot, the wind blows, the paper birls on.

Papay

And we see at last how beautiful it was, how small,
as though memory keeks down from where we never were –
the shell-sand beach, the seaweed tastefully arranged

about the lovers sprawled by rising tide,
your belly's beat absorbing mine
as though the whole shoreline were breathing.

One might think happiness a tidal island,
reached at times whose tables
don't appear in the national press.

We must leave the sickle bay
while we still can. On the sand
we stare where seals have lain –

they left a hollow, shining as it fills.

In a Bar in Lochmaddy
(for Sandy and Buzz)

You are playing dominoes against your brother, a competitive sod at the best of times. Rain snaps over Uist like a dirty mac. At the bar the shout of Gaelic is a rumour of something you once knew, now beyond reach like peace of mind or truly fluid movement. Your brother places his tile, grins, fingers his thinning hair. Keep a straight face – you've got him, you can play off either end.

The pieces in your hand are little tombstones, lichen-dotted. A lot needs said between you but not yet. An hour ago the ferry drifted from the pierhead, rolled into the mist. Happiness is never a destination, just pause before more movement – perhaps knowing that is your happiness as you ponder the final moves. He has his children and his sorrows, you can win this one.

The white-haired woman clearing tables glances at your hand then at the domino-snake. *How would you say I was doing so far?* When she looks at you, her face has the sheen of wet stones or Jim Kelman's eyes. *I'd say very well, Jim.* Which is odd because your name's not Jim. But she says it kindly, more kindly than necessary as she lays a piece across one end of the maze and leaves.

Look closer – it's not a domino but paper, an intricately folded paper form. And you've seen that hand before, your father's on your birth certificate. But this isn't your birth certificate, it is the other book-end of your life. Yet she looked so kindly, her affection seemed so real! Your eyes unfocus date and cause of death. You are not so frightened. She's left a marker, that is all.

The horizon's semi-precious, the rain is past, your brother winks and waits. Soon he must phone his children and he's built a little tower with his change. You have no children and never will. Now that one end is closed, you must re-think how to play the end-game. You hesitate. *Your go, old bro.* The malt is salty; as you sip, readiness throbs like a brave little bird in your hands.

Orkney / This Life

(for Catherine & Jamie)

It is big sky and its changes,
the sea all round and the waters within.
It is the way sea and sky
work off each other constantly,
like people meeting in Alfred Street,
each face coming away with a hint
of the other's face pressed in it.
It is the way a week-long gale
ends and folk emerge to hear
a single bird cry way high up.

It is the way you lean to me
and the way I lean to you, as if
we are each other's prevailing;
how we connect along our shores,
the way we are tidal islands
joined for hours then inaccessible,
I'll go for that, and smile when I
pick sand off myself in the shower.
The way I am an inland loch to you
when a clatter of white whoops and rises...

It is the way Scotland looks to the South,
the way we enter friends' houses
to leave what we came with, or flick
the kettle's switch and wait.
This is where I want to live,
close to where the heart gives out,
ruined, perfected, an empty arch against the sky
where birds fly through instead of prayers
while in Hoy Sound the ferry's engines thrum
this life this life this life.